The Ultimate Questions Book ~ Relationships

Copyright © 2013 Marketing Tao, LLC. All rights reserved. No part of this material shall be used for any purpose other than intended. Nor shall any part of this product or the materials included be reproduced by any means, including electronically stored, without the written permission of Kathy Jo Slusher and Marketing Tao, LLC.

The Ultimate Questions Book ~ Relationships

Table of Contents

Skillful Questioner 2
Making Questions Powerful 6
How to Use This Book 9
Additional Uses 11
Open and Closed-Ended Questions Chart 14
General Relationships Questions 15
Relationships Wheel 50
Trust & Safety Questions 51
Communication Questions 52
Boundaries Questions 55
Love Questions 57
Fun & Pleasure Questions 59
Openness Questions 61
Respect Questions 63
Interdependence Questions 65
Relationships Values / Qualities Assessment 67
Blank Wheel 69
Relationships Quotes 70
SMART Goals Checklist 75
About the Work 76
About the Authors 77
Additional Resources 78

The Ultimate Questions Book ~ Relationships

The Skillful Questioner

Problems cannot be solved by the same level of thinking that created them.
   ~ Albert Einstein

During the Renaissance there was a massive resurgence of learning and a gradual yet widespread shift in education, leading to economic growth and development, political and social reform, and an increase in trade and commerce.

The Industrial Revolution was a major turning point in human history. There were immense technological advancements, economic progress, income & population growth, and an increase in the standard of living never seen before.

Why?

They were asking themselves powerful questions that shifted the way they approached problems, and spurred curiosity and creativity.

Today, we are on the verge of another major shift. To make the leap we need to make we must ask ourselves and our clients questions that achieve & surpass that same level of curiosity and creativity.

The quality of questions we ask directly influence the knowledge we acquire and the actions we take.

By asking quality, empowering questions we can find the answers leading to the change we seek.

Being a skillful questioner is more than just the words used in the questions. It's as much about how you ask the questions as it is about the words you use. Having no attachment to the outcome of the question and addressing the questioner with curiosity, objectivity and in a non-confrontational manner creates an atmosphere of safety for the questionee to answer honestly and thoroughly.

The Ultimate Questions Book ~ Relationships

With over 30 years of coaching, training, facilitation, and experiential learning experience between the two of them, both Denny & Kathy Jo recognize even the most skilled professionals can sometimes get stuck finding the right questions.

Asking powerful questions allow the questionee to see things differently, open up creativity, gain new perspectives, see solutions, discover their own answers, deepens relationships and trust, and improves problem-solving and decision-making abilities.

You can ask the most empowering questions and unlock amazing possibilities, but unless you truly listen and the questionee feels that intent, forward movement is stunted. Listening is an important part of communication as is asking powerful questions. However, not all listening is effective listening.

It is said that hearing is a physical ability. We all hear. We don't always listen. Listening is a skill, one that must be practiced and intentional to be effective.

As a vital part of the questioning process, listening enables:
- The acquisition of new information
- Greater insight to the values, strengths, behavior and needs of the questionee
- The questionee to discover his / her own perspectives of the situation
- Trust & Rapport
- Understanding of underlying meaning
- Motivation
- Depth & Intimacy
- Mutual understanding
- The questionee to feel heard and understood

Levels of Listening

There are 4 Levels of Listening. We have all experienced listening to others and being listened to at each level. The higher the level the more energy is required to maintain that level. Not every conversation you have will take place at the Intuitive Listening level.

1. **Competitive Listening**: The main focus in Competitive Listening is on the listener's own thoughts. Here the listener is more interested in their own views and is waiting for an opportunity to jump in and react.

2. **Attentive Listening**: The main focus in Attentive Listening is on the words being said. There is genuine interest in hearing and understanding what is being said but assumes an understanding, not checking with the questionee for confirmation.

3. **Reflective Listening**: The main focus in Reflective Listening is on a deeper and clarified understanding of what is being said. There is genuine interest in listening, not just hearing, as well as understanding what is being said and confirms that understanding, often through mirroring back the exact information shared.

4. **Intuitive Listening**: The main focus in Intuitive Listening is an understanding of the meaning behind what is said. There is genuine desire to understand not only the meaning of what is being said but also the tone, pitch, speed, of what's being said, the body language that accompanies the words, what is being said behind the words, and what is NOT being said.

We all know how important communication is. However, the vast majority of communication isn't spoken. According to studies done in the '70s by Albert Mehrabian, only 7% of communication takes place through exchange of words. The remaining 93% of information is communicated through body language, eye contact, and pitch, speed, tone and volume of the voice.

Understanding that most information is not communicated through words, to be a powerful listener there are several things you have to keep in mind while listening to the questionee.

Keys to Powerful Listening

1. Intentions are set to gain a greater understanding of the questionee, their behavior, thinking, values, beliefs, perspectives and needs.
2. Stay Curious.
3. Detached Involvement: the ability to tap into deep levels of empathy and place yourself in the questionees position, understanding their thoughts and feelings without taking on their emotions.
4. Focus on what is being communicated in all areas – body language, tone, pace, pitch, energy – while not focusing on your response.
5. Offer feedback and request clarification if necessary.
6. Remember silence is golden. Don't be afraid of silence. Allow the questionee to sit with the question and ponder.
7. Use Intuitive Listening as much as possible.

When entering a conversation where you are required to deeply listen and understand questionees, try your best to enter the situation with as much energy as possible.

Powerful Questions + Intuitive Listening + Acknowledgement + Time to Respond = Unlocked Potential & Possibilities

Making Questions Powerful

Asking the right questions in the right way is key to achieving the right results. Powerful questions immediately access our creative, holistic brain, from which solutions are born. These thought provoking questions are designed to forward your client's actions through clarifying, inspiring, probing, challenging, affirming, exploring, opening new possibilities, connecting, assessing, and evaluating, leading to the right solutions for your client.

When crafting questions, there are 3 things you must consider.
1. The Scope of the Question
2. The Construction of the Question
3. Assumptions & Bias in the Question

Scope

The Scope is defined as the range or subject matter that something either deals with or to which it is relevant. The scope covers the domain of inquiry. Matching the scope of the question to meet the needs of inquiry increases the capacity to effect change and sets the questionee up for success. Therefore, keep within realistic boundaries of the situation and questionee's knowledge and power.

For example: "How can you best change your perspective?" as opposed to "How can you change the perspective within the organization?"

When determining the scope of your question you must first determine the scope of the answer you are seeking. If you are looking for greater clarification you must ask questions designed to gain that clarity. If you are looking for greater insight, you must ask questions designed to go deeper. If you are looking to at obstacles you must ask questions designed to uncover blocks. The scope of the answer determines the category of the question to achieve an appropriate response. You can find the question categories under the General Questions section of this book.

Construction

The construction of a question consists of the language, intention and tone you take when asking the question. A question's construction is a critical element in either opening up one's mind to possibilities or closing the mind to solutions. The construction of a question can determine the depth and direction of the answers. Are you looking for a direct yes or no answer? Ask a closed-ended question. Are you looking for deeper clarification? Do you want to open choices or create a new picture? Ask open-ended questions.

The construction of a question stimulates reflective thinking and deepens the conversation. Starting your question with either "who" or "how" determines the level and direction of inquiry. For example: "Who can help you to make this happen?" "How can this happen?"

When constructing the question, ask yourself what "work" you want this question to do.

Assumptions and Bias

Part of being human is that our experiences and perspectives influence the way we think. We all carry with us assumptions and biases. We cannot eliminate them. Awareness of assumptions and biases allow us to be on the look-out for them as we construct and ask our questions, and listen to the answer.

One of the most commonly used questions containing an assumption and bias is "What is wrong?" This question assumes a negative.

Reframing is a potent way to reword questions freeing them of assumptions and bias such as from "What's wrong?" to "What happened?" Reframing encourages deeper reflection and shifts assumptions into possibilities for creating forward action.

A Word About "Why"

Some of the most powerful questions begin with "Why." Some of the most dangerous questions begin with "Why."

Why-questions can lead to greater insight and more thorough answers. They ask the questionee to go deeper inside and evaluate. Answers to why-questions speak about the inner feelings, beliefs, and motives of the questionee. Because of the highly personal nature of why-questions if safely and trust have yet to be established in the relationship a why-question can easily trigger reactive behaviors and blame detracting from solutions.

The difference between getting greater insight and triggering reaction is the level of safety the questionee feels in the relationship and the way in which the question is asked.

If safety and trust have been established on both sides of the relationship and a why-question is the most appropriate question to ask, stay curious when asking your question. This will keep the non-verbal elements of asking a question as well as your intention on

Choose why-questions carefully and sparingly.

Characteristics of a Powerful Question
1. Solutions-focused
2. Clear & Simple
3. Involves Values & Ideals
4. Generates Curiosity
5. Stimulates Reflection
6. Thought-Provoking
7. Engages Attention
8. Focused
9. Touches Deeper Meaning
10. Leads to More Questions

How to Use This Book

As you encounter a specific challenge around relationships in your life or your client's life, you may become stuck and not know where to go next. This book is designed to assist in getting you and your clients unstuck by sparking new, unique, and in-depth questions. You can either use these questions as is or allow them to inspire new ideas for you.

Open / Closed-Ended Questions Chart: Open-Ended questions are designed to require the answerer to go deeper and give more detail. These types of questions should be used as often as possible to gain greater detail, inquiry, and increase understanding. Closed-Ended questions are excellent for commitment. These are used ONLY when looking for a "yes" or "no" response.

General Relationships Questions: These general Relationship-based questions are a great starting point for coaching around Relationship issues. These questions are designed around a basic coaching approach of: clarifying, creating a vision, defining choice, identifying blocks and barriers, evaluating, prioritizing, probing, and scaling. Use these questions as touchstones throughout the process. Categorized based on your client's specific needs and situation, these questions increase the scope of the coaching relationship.

Relationships Wheel: The Relationships Wheel is a self-awareness assessment you can use for yourself or your client to rate the level of satisfaction in each area of relationships. You or your client may want to broaden the scope of coaching to encompass each area and create the ideal relationship.

Wheel Specific Questions: As your coaching partnership deepens and gaps in relationship skills present themselves, you can target different areas of Relationships more in-depth through these questions. These can even prolong the coaching partnership and develop more conscious relationships.

Relationships Values / Qualities Assessment: Rating Relationships Values / Qualities by how important they are to you and how much you walk your talk can help you identify where gaps may be in your Relationship Skills. This is an excellent resource in identifying areas and opportunities for growth.

Blank Wheel: Using the Blank Wheel, fill in your or your client's top 8 Relationship Values / Qualities and rank these to address the gaps of creating the ideal Relationship. You can also develop new coaching assignments and opportunities around each area.

Relationships Quotes: This collection of Relationships Quotes is a great resource for either your own marketing efforts or to deepen the level of thinking for your clients. Use these quotes to send inspirational emails, add to your website, use as topics for your newsletters or to Tweet.

SMART Goals Checklist: SMART Goals help ensure success. Goals that are unattainable or unreasonable are a direct line to failure. Failure stifles excitement, passion, and commitment. To ensure the success of your clients, check each goal against the SMART Goals checklist to determine how viable the goal truly is and keep your client's on track.

The Ultimate Questions Book ~ Relationships

Additional Uses for This Book

Coaching / Consulting Role

→ Use the Wheel Assessment in a Complementary Session

→ Assess a client's level of satisfaction in the 8 key areas of the Relationships Wheel in an introductory session to establish the partnership foundation

→ Use SMART Goals checklist as an evaluation & progression tool

→ Create accountability around the SMART Goals checklist

→ Identify strengths & gaps in each area of the Relationships Wheel

→ Identify initial coaching goals

→ Use the questions as preparation for coaching sessions

→ Create customized assignments using the questions

→ Create visualizations & meditations based around Relationships Wheel segments or Questions

→ Use quotes in sessions to stimulate fresh perspectives

→ Add quotes to client emails for inspiration

→ Create a customized assignment by journaling on quotes

→ Create a mastermind or group discussion around a specific quote

→ Help clients set goals using the SMART Goals checklist

The Ultimate Questions Book ~ Relationships

Product & Services Development

→ Use this book and the Relationships Wheel as your Signature Program

→ Use the Relationships Wheel Assessment in a workshop as an assessment or discussion tool

→ Add the Relationships Wheel Assessment to your current Signature Program or product

→ Use questions as an idea generator

→ Create an E-course / E-book / E-workbook series around segments of the Relationships Wheel

→ Develop workshops & seminars around segments of the Relationships Wheel

→ Form Mastermind Groups around key Wheel segments

→ Use the Relationships Values / Qualities list as an idea generator

→ Write an E-course / E-book / E-workbook on a grouping of Relationships Values

→ Create Workshops & Seminars on a grouping of Relationships Values

→ Add a quote to a product or presentation for inspiration or point emphasis

→ Use quote in workshop as a discussion topic

→ Use SMART Goals checklist in a workshop as tool to move participants forward

The Ultimate Questions Book ~ Relationships

Marketing / Business Development

→ Use the Relationships Wheel Assessment as a prospect pre-qualifier

→ Create a prequalifying survey for prospects with questions

→ Use questions or quotes in ezine / newsletter

→ Post a question / quote to your target audience on a LinkedIn Discussion

→ Use a series of questions to outline a promotional teleclass

→ Create a free download of questions around a particular topic

→ Use questions in Blog & Twitter Posts

→ Write an article based on the questions

→ Write an article based on an individual Relationships Value

→ Use the Relationships Values Assessment as a pre-coaching prep form

→ Create an ezine / newsletter around individual Relationships Value

→ Post a quote on your blog / Facebook / LinkedIn asking what for comments about how it relates to the topic

→ Use a quote to inspire a podcast or video

→ Use quote to motivate article idea

→ Post Quote on Blog / Twitter

Open-Ended vs. Closed-Ended Questions

Open-Ended questions invite others to discuss in detail what is important to them. They are used to gather information, establish rapport, and increase understanding. These questions do not lead and are not geared towards expected outcomes. When used, the asker must be willing to listen and respond appropriately.

Closed-Ended questions are used to elicit a specific yes or no answer. Use only when you want a definite yes or no. They are particularly useful when determining a commitment.

Ask Open-Ended questions whenever possible.

Open-Ended Questions Start with:	Closed-Ended Questions Start with:
Who	Is
What	Does
How	Are
Why	Do
When	Will
Where	Can

The Ultimate Questions Book ~ Relationships

General Relationships Questions

Clarifying

Clarifying questions are designed to lay the groundwork and foundation for attaining goals. They set the stage, remove ambiguity, elicit details, and supply known facts.

Ask Clarifying Questions when you need a clear picture of where the questionee is currently at, what resources are available, what perspectives they have, as well as want a picture of where the questionee is coming from, what they want, and the reality of the situation.

Ask these questions as a starting point, to establish a framework.

Example of Clarifying Questions

Questionee: I want to feel more freedom in my life.

Questioner: What do you mean by more freedom?

Questionee: I mean to have the ability to do what I want when I want to.

Questioner: Give me an example.

The Ultimate Questions Book ~ Relationships

Clarifying Questions

- → Who zaps your energy?
- → Who do you rely on?
- → Who do you love?
- → Who do you fear?
- → Who irritates you?
- → Who supports you?
- → Who causes you grief?
- → Who gets in your way?
- → Who brings you up when you're down?
- → Who do you go to when lonely?
- → Who do you go to when scared?
- → Who gives you the most energy?
- → With whom is it the easiest to get along?
- → To whom do you go when you are in need?
- → To whom are you the most committed?
- → Who inspires you?
- → Who in your life do you enjoy most?
- → Who in your life shares a similar passion as yours?
- → Who makes time for you?
- → In this moment, what is the reality?
- → What do you need to understand about that person?

Marketing Tao, LLC

The Ultimate Questions Book ~ Relationships

→ What would it take to stop conflict in your relationship?
→ What would you like to see happen with this relationship?
→ What place does love occupy in your relationships?
→ What in your relationships are you most passionate about?
→ What is missing for you?
→ For what do you yearn?
→ What are you hearing this other person say?
→ What is "good enough" for now?
→ What type of situation brings out the best in you?
→ What type of person inspires you most?
→ What do you need to gain more clarity on?
→ What is the lesson that needs to be learned?
→ What have you already done to resolve this issue?
→ Where are you the most compatible with your partner?
→ Where does time stand still?
→ Where is the love?
→ Where is the understanding?
→ Where is the joy?
→ Where is the peace?
→ Where could there be more passion?

The Ultimate Questions Book ~ Relationships

- → When does teamwork succeed?
- → When does teamwork fail?
- → When does friendship fail?
- → When does parenting fail?
- → When does a partnership fail?
- → When does it succeed?
- → When does your relationship really come alive?
- → When do you have fun?
- → Why is your partner (not) happy with your relationship?
- → Why do you love him / her?

- → How social are you?
- → How do you express your love?
- → How do you express your anger?
- → How do you express your fear?
- → How would you define friendship?
- → How clear are you on what you need in a relationship?
- → How would you define partnership?
- → How would you define teamwork?
- → How would you define compatibility?
- → How do you define family?
- → How do you like to be supported?
- → How do you like to be touched?

The Ultimate Questions Book ~ Relationships

- → How do you define relationship?
- → How would you describe your family?
- → How well do you fit into your family?
- → How is friendship learned?
- → How is parenting learned?
- → How is partnership learned?
- → Without them saying a word, how can you tell someone is a good friend?
- → How independent are you?
- → How accepting are you of others?
- → How accepting are you of that person?
- → How much energy do you have for that person?
- → How do you share your passion?

The Ultimate Questions Book ~ Relationships

Visioning

Visioning questions are designed to establish a desired end result. These questions create a picture of the future so a plan on how to get there can be created.

Visioning Questions allow the questionee to "see" the result they are working to achieve. This opens possibilities, engages creativity, and keeps motivation high and direction clear.

Ask Visioning Questions when creating a new reality, establishing an end-result, identifying the ideal, or giving direction to move forward.

Example of Visioning Questions

Questioner: What would you ideally like to see happen?

Questionee: I would like to move to the country away from the noise and congestion of the city. I would like to grow my own food, and live more simply. I would like to see the stars at night and hear the crickets sing.

Questioner: In this ideal vision, what do you see yourself doing?

Questionee: I see myself writing that book I keep talking about and having time to putter around in my flower garden.

Questioner: How would you feel if you had?

Questionee: I see myself really happy, living a good life with the people I love, enjoying the things that give my life meaning.

Questioner: That is a beautiful picture for you.

Questionee: Yes it is!

The Ultimate Questions Book ~ Relationships

Visioning Questions

→ What would you change about your relationships if you could?

→ What makes you believe you are a good friend?

→ What makes you believe you are a good partner?

→ What makes you believe you are a good parent?

→ What does compatibility mean to you?

→ What do you give to your relationships?

→ What would you do if you knew you could not fail?

→ What does teamwork mean to you?

→ What makes you believe you are a good co-worker?

→ What does commitment mean to you?

→ What would it take to be a better friend / parent / partner / co-worker?

→ What does a loving partner do to show they care?

→ What do you hold back?

→ What is lacking in your relationship?

→ If you were in your advanced years and had an opportunity to tell a youngster the most important thing you learned about being a good friend, what would you tell him / her?

→ If you had to describe what a healthy relationship was in just three words, what would you say?

The Ultimate Questions Book ~ Relationships

- → What would life look like if you had perfect relationships?
- → What does being accepting of another mean to you?
- → What are your greatest hopes for your relationship?
- → What is more important in relationships, understanding or love?
- → What would a compassionate person do?
- → What would a forgiving person do?
- → What does a friend never, ever do?
- → What motivates friends to stay together?
- → What motivates partners to stay together?
- → If you had no friends, what would happen?
- → Where have you seen friendship at its best?

- → Where would you like your relationship to go?
- → Where would your family be without you?
- → Where would you be without your family?
- → How do you know when a relationship falls short?
- → How would you like to be loved?
- → How do you know when it excels?
- → How could you attract healthier relationships?
- → How much fun can you have with him / her?

The Ultimate Questions Book ~ Relationships

Choice

Choice Questions are meant to show options, empower, and accept responsibility. These questions lend to out-of-the-box thinking and demonstrate options and opportunities.

Ask Choice Questions when questionee feels trapped, hopeless, or feels as though there is no other answer, and needs a new perspective & empowerment to move forward.

Example of Choice Questions

Questionee: I don't know what to do. I really would like to attend that seminar next Saturday and Sunday but my husband wants to take the kids to the cabin that same weekend. We always do everything together.

Questioner: If you knew no-one would be upset, what options do you have to resolve this?

Questionee: You mean, if I went to the seminar and my husband took the boys to the cabin without me?

Questioner: What would happen if that could be the reality?

Questionee: Well that certainly would be different. Maybe that would work. I will talk with my husband tonight.

The Ultimate Questions Book ~ Relationships

Choice Questions

→ Whose decision is that?

→ Who is a part of your inner circle of friends?

→ For whom do you make time?

→ If you were coaching someone else in this situation, what question would you ask them?

→ If you do nothing, what will happen?

→ What are all of your choices?

→ What could you both work on that would make the biggest difference?

→ What connection is the most important to you?

→ What is the most loving thing you can do in this moment?

→ What would your relationships look like if you lived with arms wide open?

→ What if the opposite was true?

→ Where do you like to go alone?

→ Where do you like to go with friends?

→ Where do you share your true feelings?

→ Where do you hide your true feelings?

→ Where can you be of more help?

→ Where could you be more understanding?

Marketing Tao, LLC

The Ultimate Questions Book ~ Relationships

- → Where could you be more receptive?
- → Where do you need to improve as a friend?
- → Where do you need to improve as a parent?
- → Where do you need to improve as a partner?
- → Where do you need to improve as a co-worker?
- → When do you want to be social?
- → When do you want to withdraw from others?
- → When is it necessary to understand another's point of view?
- → Why would that make a difference?

- → How can you shift your beliefs about relationships to better serve you?
- → How would your family describe you?
- → How has being a friend changed you?
- → How has being a parent changed you?
- → How has being a partner changed you?

Blocks & Barriers

These questions are designed to uncover & examine what is stopping the questionee from moving forward, seeing progress, and gaining what they truly want.

Ask Blocks and Barrier Questions when you sense hesitation, resistance, goal hopping, or a belief they are unable to move forward.

Example of Blocks & Barriers Questions

Questionee: I really would like to date again but can't seem to put myself out there.

Questioner: What do you think is getting in the way?

Questionee: I'm not sure…..maybe my fear.

Questioner: Fear of what?

Questionee: Fear of not being attractive enough….of no one being interested in me.

Questioner: So you would rather stay home alone where it is safe than risk getting rejected again.

Questionee: As pitiful as that sounds, yes, I think that is it.

Questioner: How well will that work for you?

Questionee: Not very well at all since I want to meet someone! I guess we have some more work to do!

Questioner: I guess we do!

The Ultimate Questions Book ~ Relationships

Blocks & Barriers Questions

→ Who do you conflict with the most?

→ What are your greatest disappointments in your relationship with others?

→ What holds you back from expressing your love?

→ What do you bring to your relationships?

→ What beliefs do you have about yourself as a friend?

→ What beliefs do you have about yourself as a partner?

→ What beliefs do you have about yourself as a parent?

→ What beliefs do you have about yourself as a co-worker?

→ What triggers conflict at home?

→ What triggers conflict at work?

→ What triggers conflict with your friends?

→ What internal or external blocks do you have that hold you back from having satisfying relationships?

→ What is the hardest thing about relationships?

→ What is the biggest relationship challenge?

→ What makes that challenge particularly difficult?

→ Where do you limit yourself in your relationships?

The Ultimate Questions Book ~ Relationships

- → Where do you find yourself in conflict?
- → When is this relationship the least enjoyable?
- → When have you had your worst fights?
- → Why is your partner dissatisfied with your relationship?
- → Why do you get into arguments with that person?
- → How much do your thoughts affect your ability to engage with others?

Evaluating

Evaluating Questions determine criteria. They evaluate or estimate the nature, quality, extent or significance of situations. They assess factors such as needs, issues, processes, performance, and outcomes. They can also determine the cons of a situation.

Ask Evaluating Questions when the questionee needs to establish a clearer sense of their wants and needs related to a particular situation.

Example of Evaluating Questions

Questionee: I want to achieve more success at work.

Questioner: What would that look like?

Questionee: I would work more efficiently and get things done on time.

Questioner: What would be different if you were more efficient?

Questionee: I would lead meetings with more confidence and get more buy-in from the team.

Questioner: How would it feel if you achieved all of that?

Questionee: Great!

The Ultimate Questions Book ~ Relationships

Evaluating Questions

- → Who would you most like to meet? Why?
- → Who makes the best friends? Why?
- → Who makes the best partners? Why?
- → Who make the best parents? Why?
- → Who makes the best lovers? Why?
- → Who makes the best co-workers? Why?
- → Who shares your beliefs?
- → Who shares your view of the world?
- → Who would you consider to be in your "tribe?"
- → Who taught you the most about relationships?
- → Who understands you the best?
- → Who understands you the least?
- → Who do you tend to avoid? Why?
- → What does a healthy relationship look like?
- → What does an unhealthy relationship look like?
- → What effects do these beliefs have in your life?
- → What common beliefs do you and your friends share?
- → What common beliefs do you and your partner share?
- → What common beliefs do you and your family share?
- → What should a friend be passionate about?

The Ultimate Questions Book ~ Relationships

- → What should a parent be passionate about?
- → What should a partner be passionate about?
- → What should a co-worker be passionate about?
- → What is the easiest thing about relationships?
- → Where are your friendships the strongest?
- → Where have you been the most accepted?
- → Where have you been the least accepted?
- → Where are your beliefs compatible?
- → Where can you find more time for that person?
- → When are you the most compassionate?
- → When is this relationship the most enjoyable?

- → When was the last time you asked for help?
- → When was the last time you offered help to another?
- → When was the last time you befriended another person?
- → When was the last time you let someone hold you when you were sad?
- → When was the last time you were deeply moved by another?
- → When is your energy highest with that person?
- → When is your energy the lowest?
- → Why should people be friends?

The Ultimate Questions Book ~ Relationships

- → Why should families get along?
- → Why does that person love you?
- → Why would someone want you as a friend?
- → Why would someone drop you as a friend?
- → How would someone know you are in a good relationship?
- → How would someone know you are in a bad relationship?
- → How can you tell someone is a good partner?
- → How can you tell someone is a good parent?
- → How can you tell someone is a good co-worker?
- → How do power and relationships relate?
- → How can relationships take your energy up?
- → How can relationships bring your energy down?
- → How much time do you have for that person?
- → How much time do you have for your family?
- → How comfortable are you with that person?
- → How good of a parent are you?
- → How good of a friend are you?
- → How good of a partner are you?
- → How good of a co-worker are you?
- → How strong are your relationships?
- → How do you model friendship for others?
- → How do you inspire & motivate others?

The Ultimate Questions Book ~ Relationships

Goal Setting

Goal Setting Questions are designed to move into and forward the action. They include aspects of accountability, step-by-step action, and an understanding of what needs to be done in order to accomplish the desired goal(s).

Goal Setting Questions are intended to set the questionee up for success. In order to accomplish his there are certain factors to be considered when designing a goal plan.

SMART Goals help construct a format for creating successful goals.

Ask Goal Setting Questions when the questionee is ready to move into action.

Example of Goal Setting Questions

Questionee: I decided I want to return to college and finish my degree.

Questioner: That's great! When would you like to begin?

Questionee: Next semester but I have some things I need to do first.

Questioner: What do you see as the 1st step to take to get started?

Questionee: Well, I need to talk with an admissions counselor and figure out what credits will transfer and how many credits I need to complete my degree. Then I have to decide which classes to start with.

Questioner: That sounds like a plan. When will you make the appointment?

Questionee: This week. I am excited!
    (Move onto creating SMART Goals *pg.76)

Marketing Tao, LLC

The Ultimate Questions Book ~ Relationships

Goal Setting Questions

→ Who can help you do that?

→ Who else supports that?

→ With whom would you like to spend more time?

→ Who do you want to understand you more?

→ What is the hesitation about?

→ What do you want to accomplish during this session?

→ What do you want to accomplish in this relationship?

→ What is the smallest possible step you can take right now?

→ What steps do you need to take to accomplish this?

→ What is one step you can take right now?

→ What would it take for you to gain the relationships you want?

→ Where do you want your relationship to be in 6 mo., 1 yr., 2 yrs.?

→ Where would you like to go with him / her?

The Ultimate Questions Book ~ Relationships

- → Where would you like to be next year this time?
- → Where can you find more information about that?
- → When you become the type of friend you want to be, what will be different?
- → Why would your relationship end if nothing changed?
- → Why can't you live with this anymore?
- → Why change?
- → Why not change?
- → How did you do that?
- → How will you use this information?
- → How do you measure your success as a friend?
- → How do you measure your success as a parent?
- → How do you measure your success as a partner?
- → How do you measure your success as a co-worker?
- → How committed are you to that relationship?
- → How can you fill the gaps between the image of your ideal relationship and where you are currently?

The Ultimate Questions Book ~ Relationships

Prioritizing

Prioritizing Questions identifies and weighs importance, values and benefits. They can also be used to rank & order.

Prioritizing Questions are great to use in conjunction with Goal Setting Questions and can also help reduce overwhelm.

Ask Prioritizing Questions when the questionee needs to put their priorities in order or examine what is important to them.

Example of Prioritizing Questions

Questionee: I have so many things I need to get done. I feel overwhelmed!

Questioner: That is understandable considering all you have on your plate. Let's make a list of everything you have to do.

Questionee: OK.

(Together they create a list of to-do's)

Questionee: That's a lot! No wonder I feel overwhelmed.

Questioner: I hear you! Let's chunk it down. Of these 12 items, which are the most urgent and necessary to get done this week?

Questionee: I would have to say numbers 3, 6 and 7. The others can wait. I feel much better.

Marketing Tao, LLC

The Ultimate Questions Book ~ Relationships

Prioritizing Questions

→ Who are you when you're in a healthy relationship?

→ Who are you when you're in an unhealthy relationship?

→ For whom do you feel the most compassion?

→ With whom do you feel the most joy?

→ Who challenges you to be your best?

→ Who loves you unconditionally?

→ Who do you love unconditionally?

→ Who has made an impact on your life?

→ Who do you admire?

→ What are qualities and characteristics of a good friend?

→ What are qualities and characteristics of a good partner?

→ What are qualities and characteristics of a good parent?

→ What are qualities and characteristics of a good co-worker?

→ What is your top priority in a relationship?

→ What helps you feel safe in a relationship?

→ What do you most enjoy about people?

→ What do you enjoy least about people?

→ What types of relationships work best for you?

→ What is your favorite thing to do with others?

→ What are your core values when it comes to relationships?

The Ultimate Questions Book ~ Relationships

→ What qualities do best friends possess?

→ What social activity do you enjoy most? Why?

→ What social activity do you enjoy least? Why?

→ What feeling is easiest for you to express to another?

→ What feeling is hardest for you to express to another?

→ What are the top 3-5 must-haves for any good relationship?

→ With what type of person do you feel safest around?

→ What type of person brings out your best?

→ What type of person brings out your worst?

→ Where is the passion in that relationship?

→ When are you the most committed to the relationship?

→ When are relationships important?

→ When do you feel the most connected?

→ When do you feel the least connected?

The Ultimate Questions Book ~ Relationships

- → When should a relationship begin?
- → When should a relationship end?
- → When is it important to be independent?
- → Why is that important to you?
- → Why is friendship important?
- → Why is this particular friendship so important?
- → Why won't you give up on that relationship?
- → Why is teamwork important to you?
- → Why are you committed to this relationship?
- → Why would changing this relationship be important to you?
- → Why is having fun in relationships important to you?
- → How important is it to have healthy relationships?
- → How does this relationship benefit you?
- → How do you contribute to this relationship?
- → In the grand scheme of things, how important are relationships?

The Ultimate Questions Book ~ Relationships

Probing

Probing Questions make the questionee go deeper, drawing out more details, concerns, challenges, knowledge, and issues about a particular situation. A good Probing Question requires thought. These questions are used to get out the root of the situation, and reveal thoughts, feelings, and details under the surface.

Ask Probing Questions when going deeper into an issue or concern will bring greater insight and help uncover new awareness; thoughts and feelings lying below the surface.

Example of Probing Questions

Questionee: I really don't want to do my presentation tomorrow.

Questioner: Why not?

Questionee: I don't know. Even though I put a lot of time into preparing it, I guess I don't think it's very good. I'd rather hold off until I can make it better.

Questioner: From what you described last time, it appears you have a solid presentation.

Questionee: Yeah, I guess so. I just think it could be better.

Questioner: Putting the presentation itself aside, what are you really worried about?

Questionee: (Pause) That I will freeze…nothing will come out of my mouth and look like a bumbling fool!

Questioner: That is quite a worry.

Questionee: I didn't realize how anxious I am about speaking to the group.

Questioner: How would it be for us to work on that together?

Questionee: Yes, please! It would be great.

The Ultimate Questions Book ~ Relationships

Probing Questions

- → To whom do you feel the most connected?
- → Who has the greatest influence on this relationship?
- → Who are you the most open with emotionally?
- → Who are you the most open with physically?
- → Who are you the most open with spiritually?

- → Who do you feel the most selfless towards?
- → What drives you to selflessness?
- → What's fun about relationships?
- → What beliefs do you have around relationships?
- → What does independence mean to you?
- → What are your gifts as a friend?
- → What are your gifts as a partner?
- → What are your gifts as a parent?
- → What are your gifts as a co-worker?
- → What makes you feel insecure?
- → Where do you feel the most connected?
- → Where does your heart open up?
- → Where are you safest?
- → Where in your life are you feeling most threatened?

The Ultimate Questions Book ~ Relationships

- → Where is your friendship most appreciated?
- → Where can you be a friend?
- → Where do you find people like you?
- → Where can you use your friendship to make the biggest difference?
- → Where should relationships be passionate?
- → Where do you let yourself run free?
- → Where in this relationship are you most in touch with your feelings?
- → Where is the understanding you need?
- → When have you loved the deepest?
- → When have you given yourself over to another?
- → When is friendship a straight line?
- → When is friendship a curve?
- → When did you feel the best in your relationship?
- → When did you feel the worst?
- → When do you feel the most compatible?
- → When do you feel the least compatible?
- → When are you accepted for who you are?
- → When do you feel the least accepted?
- → When do you feel the most open to others?
- → When do you feel the most closed off?

The Ultimate Questions Book ~ Relationships

- → When do you feel safest?
- → When do you feel the most threatened?
- → When do you feel selfish?
- → When do you feel selfless?
- → Why do you accept that?
- → Why must you be strong?
- → How can you feel safer?
- → How connected do you feel to your partner?
- → How connected do you feel to your family?
- → How did you feel when that happened?
- → How connected do you feel to your friends?
- → How do you share your gifts with others?

New Perspectives

New Perspective Questions are designed to shift the direction of thinking. By shifting thinking the questionee can shift the way they approach the world and situations. These questions often create "aha" moments as they elicit options and possibilities previously not considered.

Ask New Perspective Questions when the questionee persists in levels of thinking that include anger, blame, victim, trapped or when they are unable / unwilling to see alternatives.

Example of New Perspective Questions

Questionee: I think my sister is upset with me.

Questioner: What makes you think that?

Questionee: Because she hasn't returned my calls this week.

Questioner: How certain are you she is upset with you?

Questionee: Well, why else wouldn't she call me back?

Questioner: Great question! What might be some other reasons she hasn't called you back yet?

Questionee: Well, maybe she's really busy with work. I know she had a big project she was working on and her boss can set some tough deadlines. I bet that's it.

The Ultimate Questions Book ~ Relationships

New Perspective Questions

- → Who would be your ideal partner?
- → If your relationship was a movie, who would the main characters be?
- → What might be a different way to think about her / him?
- → If everything was forgiven, what would be different between you?
- → What are you hoping will happen?
- → What's compelling you to reach out to that person?
- → What would be your dream relationship?
- → What is "perfect" about that person?
- → What is "perfect" about the relationship?

- → What would make this situation "more perfect?"
- → What is missing here?
- → What is the one thing you most want to have?
- → What assumptions are keeping you from trusting him / her?
- → What is limiting your ability to experience the love you desire?
- → What is stopping you from forgiving him / her?
- → What do you need to believe about yourself to have the relationship you desire?
- → If you had a magic wand in this situation, what would you do?
- → If your relationship was a force of nature, what would it be?
- → If you knew that your relationship was absolutely destined to succeed, what would you do right now?

The Ultimate Questions Book ~ Relationships

- → If your close friend was in a similar situation, what advice would you give him / her?
- → What do you think is his / her positive intention here?
- → If you could go back in time and change one thing, what would that be?
- → For what are you grateful?
- → What do you most appreciate about him / her?
- → If the room had eyes and ears, what would it see and hear when you are together?
- → What do you need in order to forgive?
- → Where is your relationship strongest?
- → Where could you see this person taking you?
    - → Where can you go with this person?
        - → Where would you like to take this relationship?
        - → Where do you enjoy your time together the most?
        - → When will you express your deepest love?
        - → When will you forgive?
        - → When have you been this excited before?
        - → When would you like this to change?
            - → When will you live wide open?
                - → When will you let go of the fear that binds you?
- → Why do you believe what he / she is saying about you?
- → Why would you let that person define you?
- → Why do you love him / her?

The Ultimate Questions Book ~ Relationships

- → Why do you fear that connection?
- → Why would someone turn their back on love?
- → Why do you desire him / her?
- → Why would this relationship make a difference in your life?
- → How far are you from that now?
- → How could you see yourself differently in this relationship?
- → How could you look at this situation differently?
- → How are those assumptions weighing you down?
- → How are those assumptions lifting you up?
- → How do you stop yourself from accepting the love he / she wants to give you?
- → How do you know that to be true?
- → How could you celebrate this new awareness?
- → If you truly believed he / she loved you, how would that change things?
- → How could you show your appreciation more fully?
- → How have you contributed to the success of this relationship?

The Ultimate Questions Book ~ Relationships

Scaling

Scaling Questions help gauge and determine the level of concern, commitment, and importance. They are a tool that identifies where the questionee would position themselves, the situation or determining a level. Scaling Questions can be used to help measure progress, attitude and behavioral change, and situational shifts.

Ask Scaling Questions when the questionee wants to gauge the level of concern, commitment, or importance of a situation or concern.

Example of Scaling Questions

Questioner: On a scale of 1-10, 1 being not at all and 10 being extremely, how important is that for you?

Questionee: I would say about an 8.5.

Questioner: That's pretty important!

Questionee: Yes, it really it.

The Ultimate Questions Book ~ Relationships

Scaling Questions

→ On a Scale of 1 to 10 (10 = excellent and 1 = terrible) where would you rank yourself as a friend? Why did you rank yourself that way?

→ On a Scale of 1 to 10 (10 = excellent and 1 = terrible) where would you rank yourself as a parent? Why did you rank yourself that way?

→ On a Scale of 1 to 10 (10 = excellent and 1 = terrible) where would you rank yourself as a partner? Why did you rank yourself that way?

→ On a Scale of 1 to 10 (10 = excellent and 1 = terrible) where would you rank yourself as a co-worker? Why did you rank yourself that way?

→ On a Scale of 1 to 10 (10 = excellently and 1 = terribly) how does this relationship currently meet your needs? Why did you rank yourself that way?

→ On a Scale of 1 to 10 (10 = not at all and 1 = everything) how much of yourself are you holding back from this relationship? Why did you rank yourself that way?

→ On a Scale of 1 to 10 (10 = absolutely and 1 = not at all) how willing are you to look at this differently? Why did you rank yourself that way?

→ On a Scale of 1 to 10 (10 = absolutely and 1 = not at all) how much do you honor yourself? Why did you rank yourself that way?

→ On a Scale of 1 to 10 (10 = absolutely and 1 = not at all) how much do you honor your partner? Why did you rank yourself that way?

→ On a Scale of 1 to 10 (10 = absolutely and 1 = not at all) how much do you honor your relationship? Why did you rank yourself that way?

Relationships Wheel

The Ultimate Questions Book ~ Relationships

Directions: for each section of the Relationships Wheel, circle the number that represents your current level of satisfaction in that area. The higher the number, the greater your level of satisfaction.

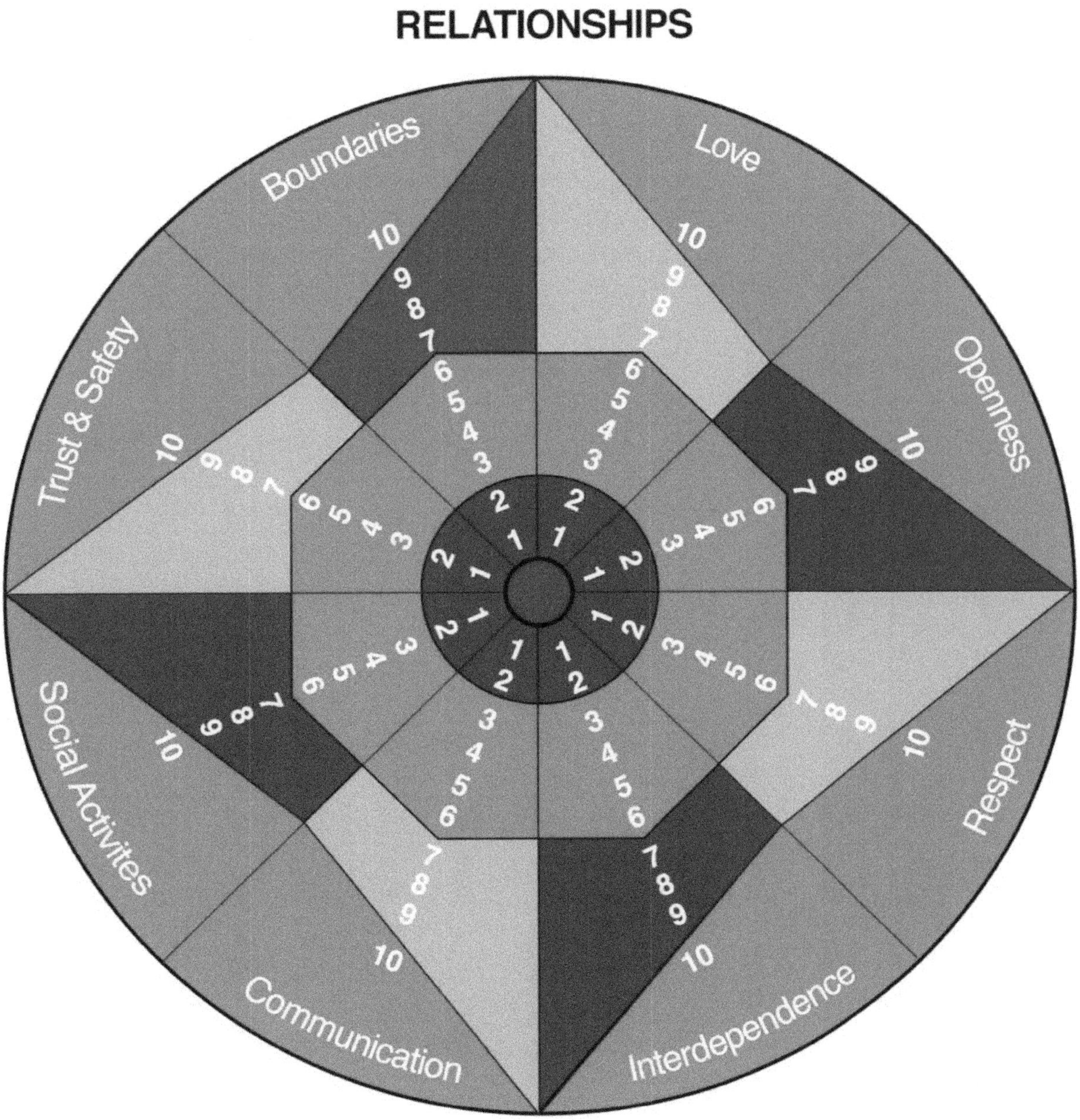

RELATIONSHIPS

Sections: Boundaries, Love, Openness, Respect, Interdependence, Communication, Social Activites, Trust & Safety

© 2013 Unaltered Reproduction Rights Granted, Marketing Tao, LLC

The Ultimate Questions Book ~ Relationships

Trust & Safety

Who
- → Who would you be without being able to trust?
- → Who do you feel safe around? Why?
- → With whom do you not feel safe? Why?
- → Who is easiest for you to trust? Why?
- → Who needs your trust the most?

What
- → What does trust mean to you?
- → What is the benefit of being a trustworthy person?
- → What is the downside?
- → What three qualities best describe someone who is trusting?
- → What could you do to become more trusting?

Where
- → Where do you feel safest in your relationship?
- → Where do you need to be more trusting?
- → Where has your trust been violated?
- → Where would your relationships be without trust?
- → Where is trust the strongest?

The Ultimate Questions Book ~ Relationships

When
- When is trust most essential in a relationship?
- When is having trust in someone a risk?
- When in the past has your trust been violated?
- When do you feel unsafe?
- When do you feel the safest?

Why
- Why is feeling safe important to you?
- Why is having someone to rely on helpful to you?
- Why do healthy relationships require trust?
- Why do people trust one another?
- Why do people lose trust in a relationship?

How
- How trustworthy are you?
- How trustworthy is that person?
- How do you know who to trust?
- How can trust be cultivated?
- How would you benefit most by having trusting relationships?

Your Questions on Trust & Safety
- _____
- _____
- _____
- _____

The Ultimate Questions Book ~ Relationships

Communication

Who

- → Who really listens to you?
- → To whom do you want to give your full attention?
- → To whom is it hardest to talk? Why?
- → With whom do you need to communicate more?
- → With whom do you need to communicate less?

What

- → What is effective communication?
- → What needs to happen for there to be effective communication?
- → What do you need to say in this relationship?
- → What do you need to hear?
- → What one thing are you holding your tongue on?

Where

- → Where does communication tend to break down for you?
- → Where are you comfortable communicating your needs?
- → Where are you not comfortable communicating?
- → Where do you need to communicate more? Of what?
- → Where do you need to communicate less? Of what?

When

- → When is the right time to listen?
- → When in the right time to speak?

The Ultimate Questions Book ~ Relationships

→ When is clear communication the hardest to achieve?

→ When does communication work best?

→ When do you feel most heard?

Why

→ Why is effective communication important in relationships?

→ Why do people need to talk?

→ Why do you need to be heard?

→ Why is clear communication sometimes difficult to achieve?

→ Why is speaking your truth essential?

How

→ How does your communication style affect your relationships?

→ How do you communicate your feelings?

→ How can you improve your communication skills?

→ How well do you listen?

→ How well are you heard?

Your Questions on Communication

→ _____

→ _____

→ _____

→ _____

→ _____

The Ultimate Questions Book ~ Relationships

Boundaries

Who

→ Who respects your boundaries?

→ Who crosses your boundaries?

→ Who can help you establish better boundaries?

→ Who do you want to let in? Why?

→ Who do you want to keep out? Why?

What

→ What does having healthy boundaries mean to you?

→ What can you do to set firmer boundaries?

→ What good are boundaries?

→ What comes to mind when you think of having a boundary crossed?

→ What do you need to change to have the boundaries you want?

Where

→ Where are your boundaries the clearest?

→ Where are your boundaries the fuzziest?

→ Where do you feel suffocated by another?

→ Where do you feel deeply connected with another?

→ Where could your boundaries be clearer?

When

→ When are your boundaries impenetrable?

→ When are your boundaries porous?

→ When do you need to have strong boundaries?

→ When do you feel safest?

→ When do you feel the most threatened?

Why

→ Why do boundaries exist?

→ Why are having clear boundaries essential to any relationship?

→ Why do boundaries get crossed?

→ Why do you want to keep that person out?

→ Why do you want to let that person in?

How

→ How do you know when boundaries are healthy?

→ How can you set a clear boundary with this person?

→ How would having clear boundaries help you?

→ How can you let that person in?

→ How can you be more flexible with this person?

Your Questions on Boundaries

→ _____

→ _____

→ _____

→ _____

→ _____

The Ultimate Questions Book ~ Relationships

Love

Who

→ With whom is the easiest for you to be intimate? Why?

→ With whom is the hardest for you to be intimate? Why?

→ Who needs your love the most?

→ Who are you yearning to love?

→ With whom can you live wide open?

What

→ What do you need to be more loving?

→ What creates barriers to intimacy?

→ What influences your decision to open up to another?

→ What would your relationship be like if love was just right?

→ What do you need emotionally or physically from him / her?

Where

→ Where do you resist expressing love?

→ Where do you need more love in your life?

→ Where can opening up emotionally help you?

→ Where do you show your love?

→ Where do you need love most?

The Ultimate Questions Book ~ Relationships

When

→ When are you afraid of intimacy? Why?

→ When are you delighted by intimacy? Why?

→ When is love most necessary? Why?

→ When do you need to be loved the most? Why?

→ When have you felt the most loved?

Why

→ Why is love important in relationships?

→ Why is love important to you?

→ Why do you sometimes shy away from intimacy?

→ Why do you feel pressured to be intimate?

→ Why is loving another so difficult at times?

How

→ How can you love more deeply?

→ How willing are you to be intimate?

→ How can you love that person?

→ How is emotional intimacy present / absent in your relationship?

→ How is physical intimacy present / absent in your relationship?

Your Questions on Love

→ _____

→ _____

→ _____

→ _____

→ _____

Fun & Pleasure

Who

→ With whom can you have the most fun?

→ Who are your joy-killers?

→ With whom do you like to hang out?

→ Who thinks you are frivolous for wanting to have more fun?

→ Who do you have to become to enjoy life to the fullest?

What

→ What is the most enjoyable thing you have ever done?

→ What is pleasurable for you?

→ What beliefs stop you from having more fun?

→ What would create more pleasure in your relationship?

→ What do you need to let go of to enjoy this relationship more?

Where

→ Where are your greatest challenges when it comes to having fun?

→ Where can you shift perspectives about these challenges?

→ Where do you need more pleasure in your life?

→ Where might you be stressed, frustrated, or worried?

→ Where might it serve you to let go of stress, frustration, or worry?

The Ultimate Questions Book ~ Relationships

When

- When do you avoid having fun?
- When do you most need to have fun?
- When do you have fun with others?
- When would be the best time to enjoy life?
- When is experiencing pleasure not appropriate?

Why

- Why is having fun important to you?
- Why do you enjoy this person?
- Why would you feel better if you had more fun in this relationship?
- Why wasn't that fun for you?
- Why have you decided you need more fun and enjoyment?

How

- How can you have more fun?
- How enjoyable would that be for you?
- How could you find more pleasure with others?
- How much fun do you want to have?
- How many fun things have you turned down?

Your Questions on Pleasure

- _____
- _____
- _____
- _____
- _____

The Ultimate Questions Book ~ Relationships

Openness

Who

→ Who tells you the truth?

→ Who lies to you?

→ To whom do you avoid telling the truth? Why?

→ Who deserves your honesty?

→ Who can hear your truth?

What

→ What is honesty to you?

→ What truth are you holding onto? Why?

→ What would complete honesty do for you?

→ From what person do you need more honesty?

→ With what person do you need more openness?

Where

→ Where can you be more open in sharing your thoughts and feelings?

→ Where would telling the truth help?

→ Where would your relationship be without openness and honesty?

→ Where can honesty take you?

→ Where can you cultivate a more open relationship?

The Ultimate Questions Book ~ Relationships

When

→ When do you need honesty most?

→ When do you need honesty least?

→ When would someone know you were telling the truth?

→ When is truth helpful?

→ When is truth hurtful?

Why

→ Why is honesty necessary in a relationship?

→ Why be honest about that?

→ Why not be honest about that?

→ Why is openness important to you?

→ Why would being open help here?

How

→ How can honesty help you?

→ How can honesty hurt you?

→ How do you rely on the honesty of others?

→ How open are you to being honest with others?

→ How often are you honest with him / her?

Your Questions on Openness

→ _____

→ _____

→ _____

→ _____

Marketing Tao, LLC

Respect

Who

- Who respects you most? Why?
- Who respects you least? Why?
- From whom do you need more respect? Why?
- Who do you need to respect more? Why?
- Who has never disrespected you?

What

- What is respect to you?
- What is the biggest benefit of respect?
- What would you do if you were fully respected?
- What taught you respect?
- What impact does respect have on relationships?

Where

- Where is respect absent in your relationships?
- Where can you be more respectful of another?
- Where would having more respect between you take this relationship?
- Where have you felt the most respected?
- Where have you felt the least respected?

The Ultimate Questions Book ~ Relationships

When
- When do you feel the most respected?
- When do you feel the least respectful?
- When does respect work best?
- When do you need respect?
- When is respect unnecessary?

Why
- Why is respect important to you in a relationship?
- Why is it hard to respect that person?
- Why do you respect that person?
- Why is it hard to show respect?
- Why would respect help you here?

How
- How often do you feel disrespected?
- How often do you disrespect another?
- How can you create greater respect?
- How can being respectful change this relationship?
- How is disrespect affecting your relationship?

Your Questions on Respect
- _____
- _____
- _____
- _____
- _____

The Ultimate Questions Book ~ Relationships

Interdependence

Who

→ Who supports you the best?

→ Who is unsupportive of your efforts?

→ From whom do you most need support?

→ Who most needs support from you?

→ With whom can you mutually create?

What

→ What does interdependence mean to you?

→ What does support look like in a relationship?

→ What relationship needs your support the most?

→ In what way does being supportive work against you?

→ What support is missing in this relationship?

Where

→ Where do you feel supported?

→ Where do you feel unsupported?

→ Where would you most like to create interdependence?

→ Where in your relationship would mutual support be beneficial?

→ Where would mutual support benefit you most?

The Ultimate Questions Book ~ Relationships

When

- → When are you most supportive?
- → When are you least supportive?
- → When does mutual support work best?
- → When are you not feeling supported?
- → When do you feel the most supported?

Why

- → Why is mutual support important?
- → Why do people support one other?
- → Why do you need support?
- → Why have you struggled with getting the support you need?
- → Why is asking for support hard for you?

How

- → How do you create interdependence in this relationship?
- → How do you give support?
- → How do you receive support?
- → How could mutual support help your relationship?
- → How can you ask for what you need?

Your Questions on Interdependence

- → _____
- → _____
- → _____
- → _____
- → _____

The Ultimate Questions Book ~ Relationships

Relationships Values / Qualities Assessment

Directions: Identify your top 8 Relationships Values / Qualities. How closely do you live these Values / Qualities?

- ☐ Acceptance
- ☐ Accountability
- ☐ Adaptability
- ☐ Adventure
- ☐ Affection
- ☐ Assertiveness
- ☐ Authenticity
- ☐ Balance
- ☐ Beauty
- ☐ Bravery
- ☐ Brotherhood
- ☐ Candor
- ☐ Character
- ☐ Clear Boundaries
- ☐ Comfort with Change
- ☐ Comforting
- ☐ Commitment
- ☐ Communication
- ☐ Community
- ☐ Compassion
- ☐ Compatibility
- ☐ Cooperation
- ☐ Courageous
- ☐ Creativity
- ☐ Dedication
- ☐ Delight
- ☐ Dependability
- ☐ Detachment

- ☐ Emotional Availability
- ☐ Emotional Intimacy
- ☐ Empathy
- ☐ Encouragement
- ☐ Endurance
- ☐ Enthusiasm
- ☐ Fairness
- ☐ Faith
- ☐ Family
- ☐ Flexibility
- ☐ Forgiveness
- ☐ Freedom
- ☐ Fulfillment
- ☐ Fun Loving
- ☐ Generosity
- ☐ Good Listener
- ☐ Gratitude
- ☐ Harmony
- ☐ Helpful
- ☐ Honesty
- ☐ Humility
- ☐ Humor
- ☐ Imagination
- ☐ Inspirational
- ☐ Integrity
- ☐ Interdependence
- ☐ Joyful
- ☐ Level-headed

© 2013 Unaltered Reproduction Rights Granted, Marketing Tao, LLC

The Ultimate Questions Book ~ Relationships

- ☐ Interpersonal Skills
- ☐ Intuition
- ☐ Listening
- ☐ Love
- ☐ Loyalty
- ☐ Mature
- ☐ Motivational
- ☐ Mutual Support
- ☐ Non-judgmental
- ☐ Obedience
- ☐ Objectivity
- ☐ Open Heart
- ☐ Openness
- ☐ Opportunity
- ☐ Optimistic
- ☐ Order
- ☐ Passion
- ☐ Patience
- ☐ Peace
- ☐ Physical Intimacy
- ☐ Play
- ☐ Playful
- ☐ Prosperous
- ☐ Protective
- ☐ Purposeful
- ☐ Reliable
- ☐ Respected
- ☐ Respectful
- ☐ Responsibility
- ☐ Routine
- ☐ Safety
- ☐ Security
- ☐ Self-Aware
- ☐ Self-Care
- ☐ Self-Esteem
- ☐ Self-Growth
- ☐ Selflessness
- ☐ Self-Regulation
- ☐ Service
- ☐ Simplicity
- ☐ Sisterhood
- ☐ Spirituality
- ☐ Spontaneity
- ☐ Strength
- ☐ Supportive
- ☐ Surrender
- ☐ Synergy
- ☐ Tactful
- ☐ Team Work
- ☐ Tenderness
- ☐ Thoughtful
- ☐ Tolerance
- ☐ Trust
- ☐ Truth
- ☐ Understanding
- ☐ Values-Oriented
- ☐ Willingness
- ☐ Wisdom
- ☐ Zeal
- ☐ _____
- ☐ _____
- ☐ _____
- ☐ _____
- ☐ _____

© 2013 Unaltered Reproduction Rights Granted, Marketing Tao, LLC

The Ultimate Questions Book ~ Relationships

Blank Relationships Wheel

Directions: in each section of the blank wheel, write in your top 8 Relationships Values / Qualities. For each section, circle the number that represents your level of satisfaction in that area. The higher the number, the greater your level of satisfaction in that area.

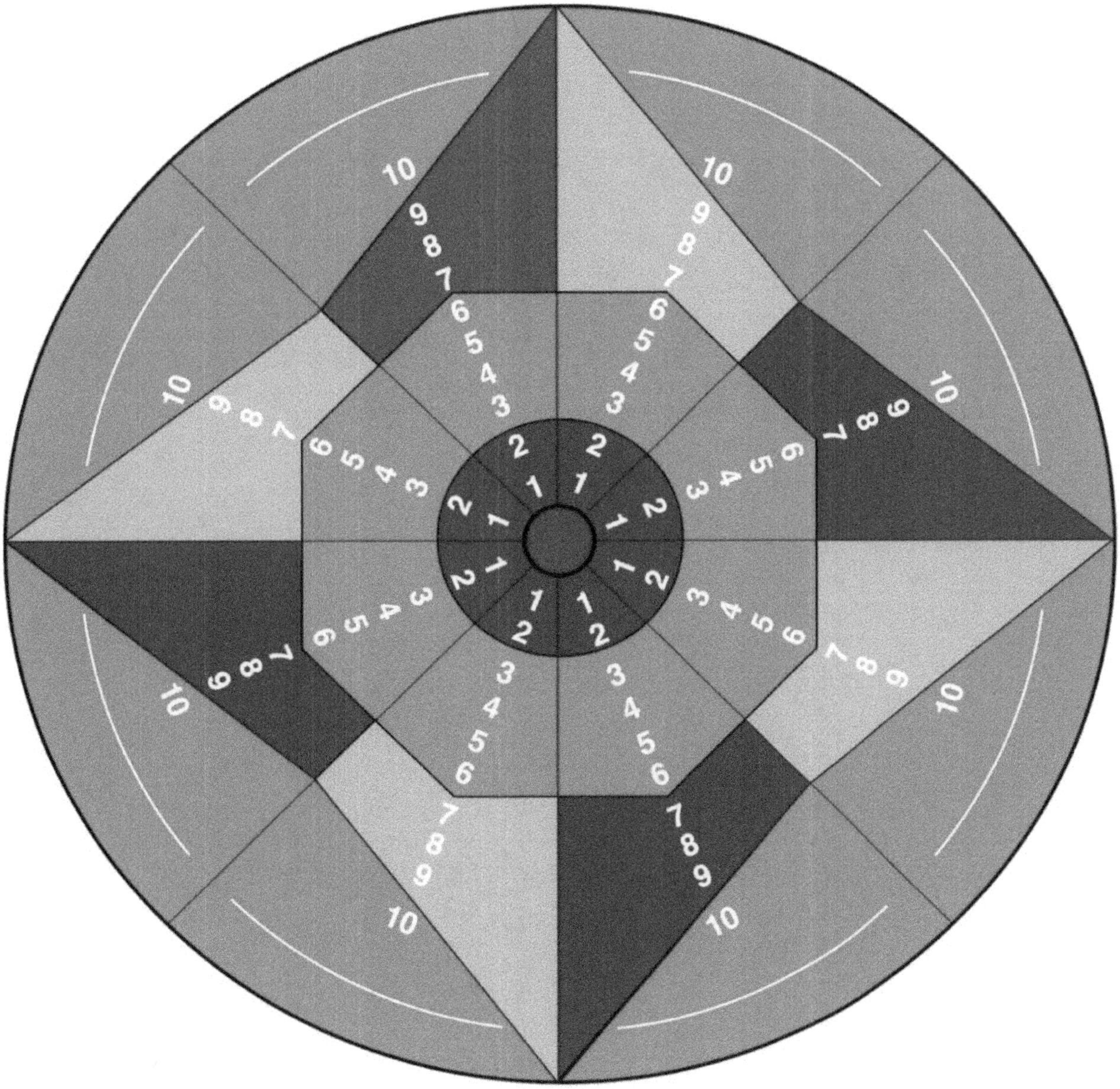

© 2013 Unaltered Reproduction Rights Granted, Marketing Tao, LLC

Marketing Tao, LLC

Relationships Quotes

When you look for the good in others, you discover the best in yourself.
~ Martin Walsh

Shared joy is a double joy; shared sorrow is half a sorrow.
~ Swedish Proverb

Trust is the glue of life. It's the most essential ingredient in effective communication. It's the foundational principle that holds all relationships.
~ Stephen R. Covey

Get the knack of getting people to help you and also pitch in yourself.
~ Ruth Gordon

Assumptions are the termites of relationships.
~ Henry Winkler

The fundamental glue that holds any relationship together is trust.
~ Brian Tracey

I like her because she smiles at me and means it.
~ Anonymous

All disagreements are results of misunderstanding someone else's level of consciousness.
~ Deepak Chopra

The quality of your life is the quality of your relationships.
~ Anthony Robbins

Your luck is how you treat people.
~ Bridget O'Donnell

Present your family and friends with their eulogies now - they won't be able to hear how much you love them and appreciate them from inside the coffin.
~ Anon

Don't rush into any kind of relationship. Work on yourself. Feel yourself, experience yourself and love yourself. Do this first and you will soon attract that special loving other.
~ Russ Von Hoelscher

The best relationship is the one in which your love for each other exceeds your need for each other.
~ Unknown

Everyone and everything around you is your teacher.
~ Ken Keyes, Jr.

Whatever my individual desires were to be free, I was not alone. There were others who felt the same way.
~ Rosa Parks

I felt it shelter to speak to you.
~ Emily Dickinson

Don't be reckless with other people's hearts, and don't put up with people that are reckless with yours.
~ Kurt Vonnegut

You can't stay mad at somebody who makes you laugh.
~ Jay Leno

One of the greatest gifts you can give to anyone is the gift of attention.
~ Jim Rohn

You can't stop loving or wanting to love because when it's right, it's the best thing in the world. When you're in a relationship and it's good, even if nothing else in your life is right, you feel like your whole world is complete.
~ Keith Sweat

Our greatest joy and our greatest pain comes in our relationships with others.
~ Stephen R. Covey

We can't help everyone but everyone can help someone.
~ Dr. Loretta Scott

To know one's self is wisdom; to know one's neighbor is genius.
~ Minna Antrim

No road is long with good company.
~ Turkish Proverb

That is always our problem, not how to get control of people, but how all together we can get control of a situation.
~ Mary Parker Follett

Do not protect yourself by a fence, but rather by your friends.
~ Czech Proverb

Let us be grateful to people who make us happy, they are the charming gardeners who make our souls blossom.
~ Marcel Proust

If enough people think of a thing and work hard enough at it, I guess it's pretty much going to happen, wind and weather permitting.
~ Laura Ingalls Wilder

People are lonely because they build walls instead of bridges.
~ Joseph F. Newton

The Ultimate Questions Book ~ Relationships

All the wealth of the world cannot be compared with the happiness of living together happily united.
~ Margaret D'Youville

Trust men and they will be true to you; treat them greatly and they will show themselves great.
~ Ralph Waldo Emerson

It is better in times of need to have a friend rather than money.
~ Greek Proverb

You cannot be lonely if you like the person you're alone with.
~ Wayne W. Dyer

No one is useless in this world who lightens the burdens of another.
~ Charles Dickens

If you judge people, you have no time to love them.
~ Mother Teresa

My only advice is to stay aware, listen carefully and yell for help if you need it.
~ Judy Blume

Cooperation is doing with a smile what you have to do anyway.
~ Anon

If we are to survive on this planet, there must be compromises.
~ Storm Jameson

We all act as hinges—fortuitous links between other people.
~ Penelope Lively

Exchange is creation.
~ Muriel Rukeyser

Keep the other person's well-being in mind when you feel an attack of soul-purging truth coming on.
~ Betty White

The smartest thing I ever did was say, "Help me."
~ Anon

"Welcome" is the best cheer.
~ Greek Proverb

Live in my heart and pay no rent.
~ Irish Proverb

That which is horrifying to you don't do to anyone else.
~ Dr. Laura Schlesinger

Great opportunities to help others seldom come, but small ones come daily.
~ Ivy Baker Priest

Forget your woes when you see your friend.
~ Priscian

Alone we can do so little; together we can do so much.
~ Helen Keller

The Ultimate Questions Book ~ Relationships

S.M.A.R.T. Goals Checklist

Specific
- ☐ What precisely is expected?
- ☐ Be as specific as possible.
- ☐ What will you have when the specific task is complete?
- ☐ What will the outcome be?

Measurable
- ☐ How would you know you have achieved success?
- ☐ How many tasks do you need to do?
- ☐ For how long?
- ☐ Make it a tangible process.

Achievable
- ☐ Is this achievable?
- ☐ What would be achievable?
- ☐ Do you have the skills or resources necessary to meet this goal?

Reasonable
- ☐ Is this a reasonable goal?
- ☐ What might be the obstacles?
- ☐ Considering everything else you have going on, can you achieve this goal?

Time-Oriented
- ☐ When will you be done?
- ☐ When will your tasks be scheduled?
- ☐ How long will it take to accomplish each task?
- ☐ When is the ideal time for this goal to be completed?

© 2013 Unaltered Reproduction Rights Granted, Marketing Tao, LLC

About the Work

We live in a time of great change. Faced with some of the most difficult challenges our world has ever known, we feel an urgency to find solutions to make our lives better. We want answers and we want them now!

In general, we focus on **getting the right answer not on asking the right questions.** Why is this? Perhaps it stems from an innate curiosity and a desire to make sense of the world. Perhaps it comes from a fear of the unknown or the need for a quick fix. It may also result from the need for blind acceptance of some *truth* where any form of questioning is strongly discouraged or denied. Perhaps we think we already have the answer, so why ask any questions at all? Whatever the case, there is no doubt human beings like answers.

When we focus on "getting the right answers," rather than "asking the right questions," we limit ourselves. We move into dualistic thinking: "I either have the right answer or I don't." We think in terms of yes or no, right or wrong, good or bad. **This black and white framework enables only surface inquiry**, at best, and quells deeper investigation and the ability to engage with others in meaningful ways. We lose the opportunity to generate new solutions to old problems.

Why are asking the right questions important? Because they generate beneficial lasting change. Empowering questions make possible diverse perspectives, which in turn lead to sustainable solutions to complicated challenges. They enable people to engage in dynamic transformational conversations out of which new ideas are born.

To generate the type of change our world needs, **we must raise penetrative questions to challenge current assumptions**; assumptions that keep us disempowered to affect change. The key in creating a positive, empowering future is asking positive, empowering questions now! So, what are you waiting for?

About the Authors

Kathy Jo Slusher, PCC, ELI-MP, Founder of Marketing Tao, LLC, has dedicated her life to help service-based socially conscious business owners make their business a success through sharing their passion. She believes that when your intention is on your passion and helping others, money is a natural bi-product. *It's not what you sell but what you stand for that makes you a success*. She is deeply committed to helping soloprofessionals and small business owners implement mindful marketing techniques and strategies to attract their ideal clients while making a difference in the world.

Kathy Jo is a Co-Founder of The REAL Results Coaching Exchange, partner in Coaching Skills for Leaders, a member of the International Coach Federation, and Vice-President of the United Nations Association of the US, Indianapolis Chapter.

Denny Balish, PCC, ELI-MP, Professional Certified Coach and Founder of ThreeFold Life Coaching, has dedicated her life's work to the development of Human Potential. She believes that each person has within themselves the desire and ability to be a positive force for change in the world and, by sharing one's unique gifts and talents with others, global change is possible. Denny is deeply committed to helping people and organizations get and stay powerfully on-purpose so they can be the change they wish to see in the world. Denny is a member of the International Coach Federation (ICF), Association for Global New Thought (AGNT), and founding board member of Spirit's Light Foundation, an alternative youth and family ministry with the Association of Unity Churches International.

Other Valuable Resources

For Coaches, Consultants, and Service-Based Small Businesses

 **Ultimate Questions Books**

The real power in transformation is not in the answers, but in the questions we ask. If coaches, therapists or consultants are unsure of the questions to ask, client results are greatly impacted.

This series of books is specifically designed for coaches, consultants, therapists and others who are in a place where they need some fresh ideas to get themselves, a client, or anyone else unstuck. www.UltimateQuestionsBook.com

 **Marketing Made Practical**

Marketing Made Practical is a Home Study Program designed for those who are overwhelmed with all the options and don't have a handle on how to make the marketing process into an effective, successful strategy.

Marketing Made Practical is specifically designed for service-based soloprofessionals or small business owners who are just getting started or have a limited experience and need an organized approach to marketing. www.MarketingMadePractical.com

 **Marketing Strategies University**

Marketing Strategies University is an online training program that walks you through how to create a strong marketing and business development plan.

Marketing Strategies University cuts to the chase of marketing. We don't dive into the theory of marketing – but focus on practical steps to create and implement powerful marketing strategies. This unique online training program is designed for service-based soloprofessionals or small business owners who have reached a certain level in their business where they are ready to create the systems and strategies for their marketing to take them to the next level of success. www.MarketingStrategiesUniversity.com

Marketing Strategies Success

Marketing Strategies Success is an online membership forum which brings together motivation and information into a community of like-minded business owners all working to create change through their business.

Through topic specific open Q & A calls & recordings, to an interactive forum where members share ideas, to a mentoring component of Success Stories, where successful entrepreneurs share their success secrets, this group will help those who have a message to share through their business but need marketing know-how & structure to accomplish their mission. www.MarketingStrategiesSuccess.com

For Leadership Development Support

Coaching Skills for Leaders

Employees don't leave companies, they leave managers.

According to the Gallup Poll, 71% of employees studied said they were either not engaged or actively disengaged at work. This employee disengagement results in $370 Billion lost annually. That's a huge amount.

In today's environment, talented individuals are arguably an organization's most valuable resource. Yet studies show, high potential employees have a higher turnover rate than any other employee population.

Leaders need to be flexible, adaptable, creative and resourceful to deal with the reality of our economic times. Coaching Skills for Leaders will take you and your organization through The Coaching Clinic, a specialized training program where you acquire a new approach to old issues. This process offers a step-by-step process to a coaching conversation in how to conduct & lead those difficult conversations. You will learn how to address organizational challenges through a step-by-step structured approach to facilitate your own coaching conversation, and develop partners and accountability standards across the board. Thus you will be transforming managers into true Leaders. www.Coaching-Skills-for-Leaders.com

The Ultimate Questions Book ~ Relationships

 ## Lifestyle, Leadership, Legacy

What are you working for?

As a business owner or executive you've worked hard to get where you are at. But how has this helped the lifestyle you want to lead? If you're tired to living to work instead of working to live, this program is for you.

We will identify your desired lifestyle, look at how to improve your leadership ability so you can more effectively lead those around you as well as your own life and create a lasting legacy to leave behind.

 ## On-Purpose Leadership Development

For on-purpose professionals who want to develop their leadership acumen while expanding their consciousness. This program formulates a plan of action to break through all obstacles limiting your success, while building powerful skills to help you lead with purpose, including: manage conflict and chaos with greater ease, use your intuition for effortless decision-making, communicate effectively and persuasively, maximize your ability to engage and influence people in positive ways, and feel empowered to affect change in yourself and others.

The Ultimate Questions Book ~ Relationships

For Specialized Support for Non-Profits, Social Enterprises and Cultural Creatives

 ### Life Purpose Coaching

Empowering individuals in their midlife years to create a life of deeper meaning and purpose by not only connecting with their authentic voice and innate wisdom, but also by helping them aligning their skills, talents and interests with their desire to give back in meaningful ways.

 ### On-Purpose Career Transition

For individuals in all phases of career and job transition who seek to purposefully align their skills and abilities with their passion for a satisfying career; one that enables them to give back in meaningful ways. Make a living while making a difference! This program is customized to fit individual needs.

For More Information Contact:

Marketing Tao, LLC
Kathy Jo Slusher
Email   info@MarketingTao.com
Call   317.536.5544
Click   www.MarketingTao.com
Click   www.TheREALResultsCoachingExchange.com

Threefold Life
Denny Balish
Email   info@threefoldlife.com
Call   708.209.6977
Click   www.Threefoldlife.com

www.ingramcontent.com/pod-product-compliance
Lightning Source LLC
Chambersburg PA
CBHW081217230426
43666CB00015B/2769